WELLINGTON'S

Wellington Shreds (and Patches)

Allan Frost

Published by Wellington Civic Society

The right of Allan Frost to be identified as the Author of this work has been asserted in accordance with the Copyrights, Designs and Patents Act 1988.

All rights reserved.

No part of this book may be reproduced or transmitted in any form or by any means, electronic or mechanical, including photocopying, recording or any information storage and retrieval system, without permission in writing from the publisher.

This book is sold subject to the conditions that it shall not, by way of trade or otherwise, be lent, re-sold, hired out or otherwise circulated without the publisher's prior consent in any form of binding or cover other than that in which it is published and without a similar condition including this condition being imposed on the subsequent purchaser.

© Allan John Frost 2006

ISBN 0 9520173 5 0
978-0-9520173-5-6

British Library Cataloguing in Publication Data:
A catalogue record for this book is available from the British Library.

Published by Wellington Civic Society
18 Barnfield Crescent, Wellington, The Wrekin, TF1 2EU, England.

Acknowledgments

Author's collection
George Evans
Ironbridge Gorge Museum Trust
M. McCrea
B. Morris
Shropshire Archives
Shropshire Star
D. Treherne
Wellington Journal & Shrewsbury News
Wellington Library
Wellington Standard

Contents

Introduction	5
1. The Wellington Journal	7
2. The Wellington Standard	15
3. R. Groom, Sons & Co. Ltd	23
4. Officialdom in 1889	31
5. Pictures from the Past	39

Illustrations inside covers
Front: Details of miscreants sentenced at Wellington magistrates' court during 1889.
Rear: Wellington trade advertisements from 1889.

Work gets under way to convert the overgrown and unkempt All Saints parish churchyard into a tasteful Garden of Rest as part of the town's Queen Elizabeth II Coronation celebrations, 1952.

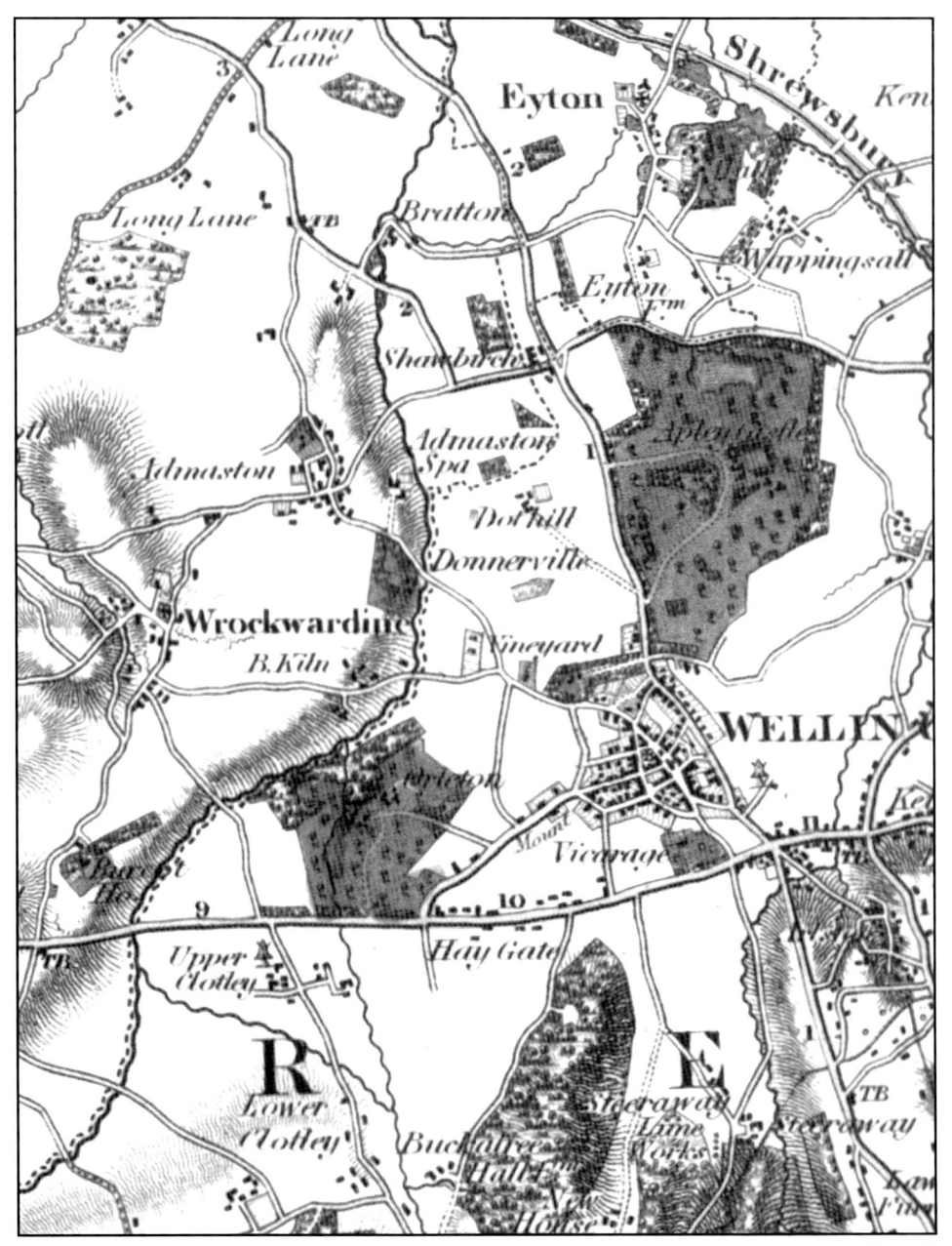

Map of Wellington, 1826. Note the windmill below the 'E' of Wellington and the 'Umbrella House' Toll Booth ('TB') towards bottom left. Many major roads were maintained by turnpike trusts at that time.

Introduction

I have attended Wellington Civic Society's monthly meetings for the last few years. It came as something of a surprise when, towards the end of 2005, President George Evans announced that he would no longer write any further books on the town's past. Since the Society relies for a portion of its income on sales of George's popular publications, I felt concerned that the important work of the Society might be adversely affected. So I decided to help by producing this book purely to help their funds.

The book contains material which would not otherwise be included in my other publications, plus additional information which was received too late for inclusion in previous books. It all makes for interesting reading and will, hopefully, give a better understanding of past conditions and activities in the town. With a bit of luck, it might encourage others to lend me material, without which the business of research is severely hindered. Better still, it might inspire them to publish their own research. No one can know everything and there is always room for new writers with a genuine interest.

Like George, I grew up in Wellington. I'd like to say I was born here but, as there were likely to be complications with my birth, my mother was taken to the hospital at Cross Houses near Atcham where her confinement could be properly supervised. So, I can honestly say I was born in a Workhouse, for that is what the hospital had been in former times, as had the Wrekin Hospital in Wellington.

Also like George, and we are definitely not alone, I have developed very strong feelings of affection and loyalty towards Wellington. It am frustrated to see how the Borough of Telford and Wrekin Council seems reluctant to acknowledge the rich, characterful histories and appearance of the old townships which it is elected to represent and promote. The same applies to Ironbridge which, while of historic importance, is a relative newcomer to the district and, regretfully, has become little more than a tourist theme park whose historic relevance has been compromised. The Ironbridge museums undoubtedly bring money into a few parts of the local economy but wouldn't it be of greater advantage in the long term to support established townships and spread the income across the wider community by encouraging visitors to explore elsewhere within the borough?

Successive Councils have demolished many of the town's historic buildings over the last 60 years without any real regard for the impact on Wellington generally or its people and businesses in particular. Planners of previous years appear to have shown a regrettable tendency to remove many traces of the past, replacing them with nondescript buildings, questionable road layouts, etc.; furthermore, they expected the public to pay for them without question, and dug their heels in if questions were raised. To me, it seems a classic case of the tail wagging the dog. Whether the Borough's councillors learned any lessons from the debacle of imposing car parking charges on the fragile economies at Newport and Wellington during 2004 and 2005 remains to be seen, as do future planning decisions.

Many people have become interested in the colourful history of the area, including 'newcomers' over the last thirty or so years who are now discovering just how much of our heritage has been lost in such a short space of time.

There's far more to the Telford conurbation than Ironbridge and a central shopping mall. Wellington, like Dawley, Oakengates, Madeley, Hadley and other towns within Telford, deserve better. Their histories are individually unique, yet collectively intertwined. One would have difficulty surviving without the others. There is so much the Borough Council could do to encourage visitors into the overall area so that, if nothing else, tourists can understand that Ironbridge was a product of wider local circumstances than an isolated historical abberation.

Wellington has a very long past and has always served the needs of surrounding districts without giving preferential treatment to any one settlement. With a little common sense, it should have a very long future. There is still a great deal to uncover of the town's past, so please spread the word by encouraging others to take an interest, particularly local councillors.

Read on, and discover a few more fascinating things about this historically rich town. And, if you value the preservation of the past and have concerns about what is happening now or may happen in the future, support Wellington Civic Society!

A Wellington Journal & Shrewsbury News *photograph of 1st Wellington Guides at their social evening in December 1950 during which they performed scenes of campfire ghosts and a burlesque on Guide activities. Front, from left to right: Iris Stanyon, Grace Davies, Janet Watterson. Rear: Eileen Bellingham, Margaret Yapp, Judy Peplow, Joy Stanyon, Norena Newnes, Cynthia Bellingham, Ann Birch.*

Chapter 1

The Wellington Journal

Local newspapers succeed because they cater specifically for the interests of those who live in their circulation area. People like to read items to which they can relate. They are familiar with the locality and derive information from a wide variety of articles, especially those concerning births, marriages, deaths, social and political events and disasters. Newspapers are also a useful means of advertising, whether for jobs, goods, services and, especially in times of war or domestic upheaval, passing on important information. If it's worth knowing, it will be found inside the pages of a local newspaper.

The nineteenth century witnessed the appearance of countless local newspapers. Some, like the *Wellington Journal*, catered both for the needs of the farming as well as urban community. Wellington was, until the demise of its famous Smithfield in 1989, essentially a market town. The *Wellington Journal* was not, however, the only newspaper serving the district; several more came and went, forced to fall by the wayside because of competition or taken over by and absorbed into the *Wellington Journal* itself as they posed a threat to the *Journal's* own existence. Among those succumbing to the *Journal's* power and influence were *The Shropshire News & Mineral District Reporter, Eddowes's Shrewsbury Chronicle, The Shropshire Guardian & Shropshire Herald* and *The Shropshire Evening News*. It was a cut-throat world. Ultimately, *The Wellington Journal & Shrewsbury News* (as named when it ceased production in 1965) was itself absorbed within the Shropshire Newspapers group based at Ketley, where the daily *Shropshire Star* is produced along with numerous other titles of newspapers and magazines.

The Wellington Journal & Shrewsbury News still holds a place in the hearts of Shropshire's older residents, not just for the quality of its reporting and range of articles but also because it is the prime source of information for historians and family researchers. Fortunately, copies have been microfilmed by the British Library and are available for viewing at certain libraries in the county.

However, the accuracy of reports cannot always be relied on. As with many newspapers, the owners (and, consequently, their editors) hold a particular set of views and opinions which can influence the style, content and bias. This is quite noticeable in reports made during, for example, the late 1880s and early 1890s, when articles in the rival *Wellington Standard* (see next chapter) cast an entirely different light on certain events. The *Journal* was the voice and vehicle of The Establishment in the town. Its owners dined and socialised with that august body of self-important men who sought public office and supposedly served the town and its inhabitants. Some were more liberal-minded than others but the *Journal* knew where its loyalties lay. Time, however, has the effect of changing traditional views and the *Journal* was obliged to recognise that fact.

As a researcher, the author is frequently surprised by the quality of photographs taken by *Journal* photographers as long ago as 100 years. Sadly, most, if not all, of the old negatives (on glass as well as celluloid) were lost or destroyed during the move from the *Journal* offices in Church Street to the *Shropshire Star's* new offices at Ketley in 1963. *(If anyone has old* Journal *prints or negatives, please get in touch with the author before they're lost forever!)* They represent a valuable source of information. Journal photographers didn't just take photographs for the newspaper; they were also hired by individuals and organisations to take private photographs for a modest fee.

The first issue of *The Wellington Journal* was produced in January 1854 by Thomas Leake, a printer in the town. Initially a six-page monthly publication costing one penny, it became a weekly newspaper with (by 1864) a circulation of 4,550 copies. The size increased to eight pages in 1866 and the circulation rose to over 10,000 copies by 1874. Such a rise in demand led to Mr. Leake investing in new machinery in 1877 to cope with demand.

Thomas's two sons, Thomas Shaw Leake and Charles Whitford Leake, joined the firm after being trained in London and took control following their father's death in 1883. Circulation continued to rise, requiring more modern presses. By 1911, the paper had a further six pages and a circulation of over 40,000 copies per week distributed throughout Shropshire.

Thomas and Charles retired in 1919 and 1924 respectively, leaving the way clear for their own sons to continue running the business. They formed Leake Ltd, a private company with four sons as directors and Charles continuing as general manager and advisor. While the price had risen to a penny-halfpenny in 1920, no further increase was made until 1937 (although the number of pages rose to twenty in 1927), when it rose to twopence to cover higher production costs. The price rose again to threepence in 1942 when the number of pages had to be reduced because of wartime restrictions and newsprint rationing. The situation improved in the 1950s when rationing ceased and Victor G. Leake was managing director.

It was a sad day when the last copy rolled off the presses in February 1965; weekly circulation had risen to some 50,000. Production, under various local editions of the *Shropshire Journal,* continued for a while but these failed to create the same enthusiasm. The closest publication to resemble the former *Journal* is the *Telford Journal,* a free weekly newspaper. Unfortunately, it has been forced by economic necessity to rely heavily on selling advertising space to the detriment of its reporting content; nevertheless, it continues to record at least some of the district's events and activities which will prove invaluable to future historians and family researchers, although not so comprehensively as the wonderful *Wellington Journal.*

Top: Journal *masthead from a 1934 issue.*

Above, *from left to right: Thomas Leake, Thomas S. Leake, Charles W. Leake, Victor G. Leake.*

Below:*Entrance to* The Journal *office on the corner of Church Street (left) and Queen Street, 1950s.*

Journal *Public Office* with its corner doorway onto the street, 1958.

The Front Office, 1958. From left to right: George Brown, Andy Leech, Horace Bagley. Note the old gas lamps contrasting with modern strip lighting.

Paper supplies being delivered via the Queen Street side entrance to the printing works, 1958.

The Paper Store, 1958.

Typesetting using lead, 1958. Typesetting on the 'stone' are (from left to right) Eric Howley, Roly Jones, Cyril Bowdler, Reg Vaughan.

Typesetting on Linotype machines, 1958, with Bill Tidman, Tommy Deakin and Stan Jones.

Plate making using the Pony Autoplate, 1958, with (from left to right) Johnny Williams, Les Treherne, Bill Parton.

Henry Morgan (background) and Graham Jones in the Print Room, 1958.

Press Room, 1958. From left to right: Les Treherne checks the print quality of the papers, Johnny Williams at the wheel monitoring the press, David Groucott and Henry Morgan.

Above: Thursday evening in the Despatch Room, 1958. Alf Walker stands in the doorway. Others include Andy Leech, George Brown, David Groucott, Cyril Woolf and Johnny Bethel.
Below: Journal delivery van, 1958. From left to right: Messrs. Treherne, Osbourne, Parton and Parton.

Soldiers read The Wellington Journal & Shrewsbury News *on the corner of Church Street and Queen Street during the Great War. Pages from the latest issue were posted in the office window specifically for soldiers to catch up on the latest news. The general public also took advantage of the situation.*

**WELLINGTON JOURNAL AND SHREWSBURY NEWS
SEPTEMBER 30, 1963**

J. E. Rickett, S. G. P. Jones, J. E. Jones, A. E. Palin, J. S. Williams, G. L. Parton, C. W. Woolf, J. G. Bethell, G. S. Jones, F. E. May, P. B. Byram, F. Harrison, D. A. Schofield, W. H. Quayle, P. J. Love.

T. Blocksidge, J. T. Dromgool, W. Bishton, M. G. Jones, H. Morgan T. E. M. Sockett, W. E. Tidman, T. A. Baker, E. James, R. T. Jones, T. Deakin, F. R. Fuller, R. Brock.

W. A. Lockley, W. Dumbell, B. L. Morris, R. Allan, A. H. Walker, F. Worsley, Miss P. Davies, Miss L. J. Foulkes, Mrs. F. Coe, Miss V. E. Dyer, Miss J. A. Roberts, Miss L. J. Hanson, Mrs. H. C. Grigg, Miss L. E. Clee, Mrs. E. Hayward, Miss C. E. F. Thomas, W. E. Newman, J. D. Davies.

F. C. Nicholas, S. R. Hall, W. J. Shorter, L. W. Osborne, L. Treherne, G. E. Brown, Mr. T. G. Leake, Miss E. E. Leake, Mr. G. B. Leake, Mr. A. Woolley, Mr. R. V. Leake, R. J. Vaughan, J. E. C. Lewis, H. Bagley, A. Leech.

D. H. Bates, M. Rowley, R. J. Smith, G. J. Mervill, P. Richards, J. Herring, R. Tranter, D. J. L. Elderwick, P. H. Hayward, J. Davies.

Journal *staff seen at their last day in Church Street, 30th September 1963.*

Chapter 2

The Wellington Standard

The Wellington Standard was just one of several newspapers competing against the *Wellington Journal*. It appears to have been printed between April 1887 and December 1891. Like the others, it failed to survive, partly because it expressed liberal views, very popular with small shop keepers and downtrodden lower classes but regarded as subversive by those wishing to keep a firm hold on the Established Order of narrow-minded Victorian values... and power. The motley collection of well-heeled, self-important influential Wellington businessmen who sat on several boards and controlled all aspects of the town's government and development, showed remarkable and unforgivable insensitivity when it came to spending ratepayers' money.

The Wellington Standard sank into undeserved oblivion (a process speeded up by an understandable lack of advertising support by those it felt obliged to criticise); surviving copies shed an alternative light on events affecting the town which, given that the *Wellington Journal* was, during the 1880s and `90s at least, very much an organ for promoting the opinions of the town's elite, help to give a more balanced view.

Here are a few articles worth repeating, taken from editions issued during 1889.

* * * * *

Wellington has had its fair share of unusual visitors over the years, most of whom were engaged in selling goods on market days or providing entertainment. This article, reported in January 1889, reveals information about just one of them:

PRINCE BULGOW

I came across some reference in a trade journal the other day to an individual who used to attract much attention in Wellington on market days. Where he is now I cannot say, for he has vanished from the horizon hereabouts. The personage to whom I allude was no less an identity than the Prince Bulgow, the great Ornate Chief of the Fiji Islands.

'His get-up was unique. The first time that I saw him he made a great impression on me,' says one of the fraternity amongst whom he moved. He was a somewhat good-looking copper-coloured native about middle height, with a ring in his nose, and large brass rings in his ears, dressed up in new breeches and low shoes, with a waistcoat of Josephean hues, adorned with imitation pearls and huge beads about his head and neck, wrists and arms, twenty or thirty brass rings upon his

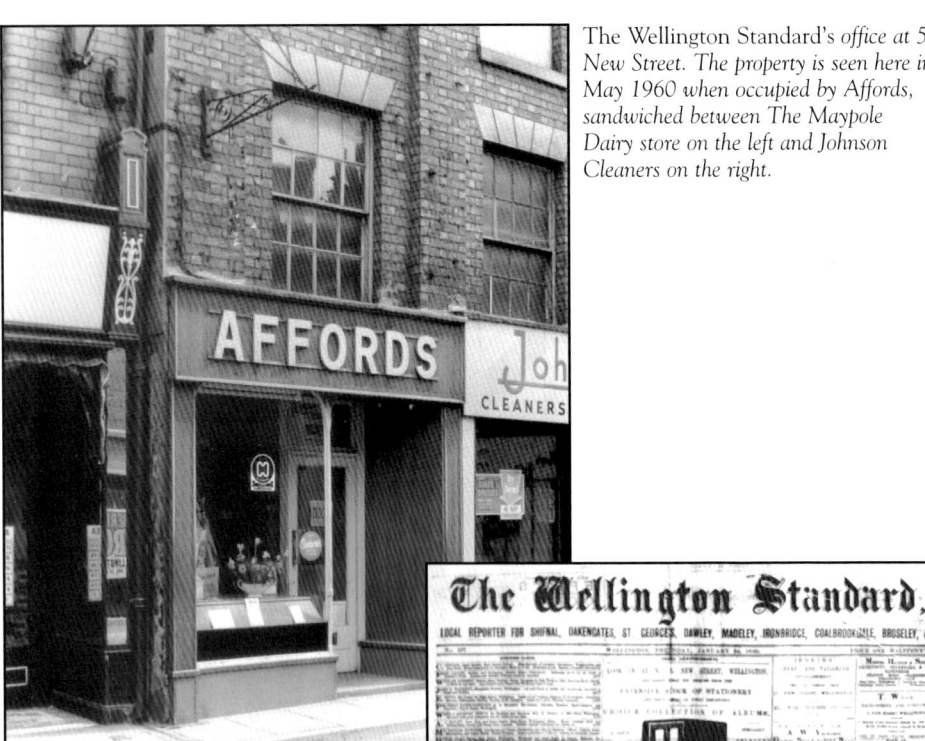

The Wellington Standard's *office at 5 New Street. The property is seen here in May 1960 when occupied by Affords, sandwiched between The Maypole Dairy store on the left and Johnson Cleaners on the right.*

The front page from one of the January 1889 issues of The Wellington Standard. *The newspaper comprised six pages and wound up its operation in less than six years. During that time, however, it managed to make a valuable contribution to a more liberal approach to newspaper reporting by taking into account the views of traders and the working classes.*

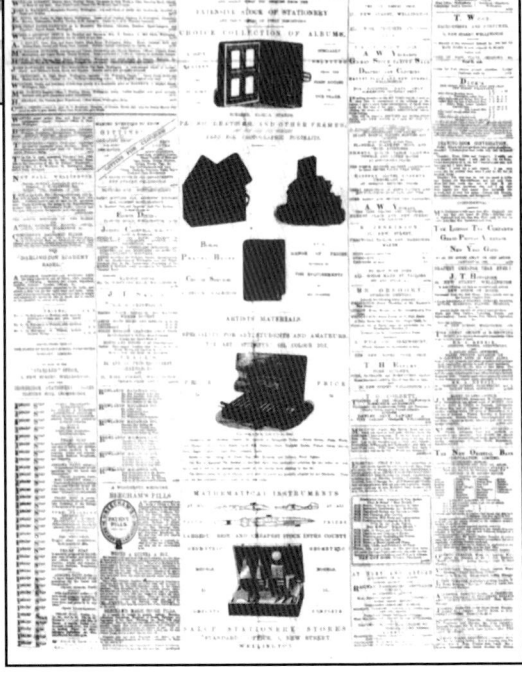

fingers and a turban of similar material. Truly a remarkable medicine vendor!

Years ago he used to exhibit himself in penny shows at fairs; but in after life he turned his thoughts to medicine. He carried a little round box, which contained his several pills... pills for fits, and pills that acted, as he was in the habit of saying, upon the 'disorganisation.'

His appearance always attracted the attention of the country people all round the Wrekin, and in time he became as familiar at Bridgnorth, Wellington, Oakengates &c., as market days. What tales he used to tell! He was a prince in his own country, and studied medicine in some college in Peru, from whence he first brought the snuff that made him so famous.

'Everybody,' he would say with a touch of pride and declamation. 'Has had Bulgow's snuff. Everybody should try Bulgow's famous pills.' His pills were made up for him by an old herbalist at Hanley, and from him one may judge that he learnt what little knowledge he possessed, if such a modicum of learning can be called knowledge.

'I met the Prince once in a small country village,' says his friend before quoted. 'And I proposed a drink, to which he assented. We had no sooner entered the public house than the landlady, a delicate woman, fell down in a swoon at his peculiar barbaric appearance; and it was many weeks before she got over the shock.

Anyone could buy a box of Chief's pills for a modest sum of 3d, or a similar lot of snuff for 1d. Had he only had a grand turn-out, with equipage and livery servants, no doubt this Prince of the Cannibals would have been a great success, for he is thoroughly believed in even now by many of the country people who come to Wellington and other towns on market days, and miss his sable presence.'

* * * * *

This critical article would be regarded as politically incorrect if it appeared in print today yet, despite mentioning the word 'darkie', which continued to be used in a descriptive rather than derogatory fashion until well into the 1960s (and possibly beyond by older residents of the town), there is no hint of racism:

O.O.O.'s

After a silence, I am told, of six years, the 'O.O.O.' Minstrels, a troop of darkies hailing from the county town, appeared in Market Hall, Wellington, on Monday evening last. There was not a large audience present, but this, perhaps, was only to be expected from the scanty manner in which the affair had been advertised, and it was certainly not to be regretted in the interests of the Wellington public.

The O.O.O.'s have evidently slumbered for the six years they have been in retirement; at least, this is the only hypothesis upon which I can account for their producing such a catalogue of stale jokes and worn-out melodies. It is really too bad to hear the cheap wit that has become the property of the street, and the airs that have been ground out of barrel organs for the last half-a-dozen years, reproduced at a public entertainment. To be bright, crisp and witty is surely the first duty of a minstrel troupe. A friend of the O.O.O.'s remarked to me that they were absolutely nothing at all, if they were not original.

There was certainly not a scrap of originality about their performance, and I leave it to their friend to do the sum. Three ciphers, minus originality, does not stand for very much.

However, the *Standard* was gracious enough to apologise when the O.O.O.s returned to perform again in Wellington:

I have to apologise to a troupe of local darkies who gave an entertainment to the town on Easter Tuesday for not noticing their performance before but, owing to circumstances of an altogether unforeseen character, these notes were crowded out of our last issue together with the criticism in question. However, better late than never, and I hasten to make good the omission.

From first to last the proceedings were an unequivocal success; the house was bumper full; and all the songs and selections were really first-rate. For a troupe of beginners they acquitted themselves in a manner that won them hosts of admirers, and to wind up in the orthodox manner I cannot do better than say that, as all the contributions were so uniformly excellent, it would be invidious to particularise.

* * * * *

The *Standard* seldom failed to say what was on everyone's mind when certain events were reported:

GILBERT GRACE

A young gentleman who rejoices in the name of Gilbert Grace and, in addition to claiming to be the son of a previous vicar of Wellington, also assumes to himself the right of training up the youths in his father's present parish in the way they should go, has just succeeded in making himself supremely ridiculous in the eyes of all thinking people.

This paragon of the amenities and requirements of the social life of youth recently compelled a boy to go down on his knees and beg his pardon for presuming to pass him without raising his hat; and when the boy's mother went to the vicarage to expostulate at the young hopeful's conduct, Master Gilbert produced an argument in support of his conduct, more forceful than convincing, in the shape of a horse-whip, which he applied to the woman's legs. Police Court proceedings were taken, and in the result, Master Grace was fined.

All this, of course, came to the public ear in due course; and, thinking to whitewash himself, Master Gilbert has written to say that what he did to the boy was only done in fun, and that he only whipped the mother's petticoats and did not hurt her legs.

The ideas of fun which Master Grace possesses are certainly rather novel ones; and if the magistrates who tried him had entertained similar ones and, just in fun, you know, ordered him to be soundly birched, they would have been supported by all lovers of fair play.

* * * * *

Even the smallest things interest the public. They always have and always will. Today, we take so much for granted and rely on television to keep us informed about and amused with the most inconsequential and banal items that it is easy to forget how mundane life was for folk living in late Victorian times. Anything even slightly out of the ordinary was reported so that readers could witness things for themselves or be made aware of them. As the town was relatively small, most of its inhabitants knew their neighbours and avidly read all reports of human interest, especially those concerning personal injury or misfortune. Religion, too, was an important aspect of many people's lives.

A BIG FISH

One of the largest, if not the largest, salmon, that has ever been pulled out of the Severn, has been on view at Mr. Bowering's shop in New Street, Wellington.

It is 4 feet 6 inches in length and measures 27 inches round the middle. It weighs 60lbs and is one of four salmon caught in the Tern Pool by Mr. T. E. Allen, who sent it to Mr. Shaw, High Street, Shrewsbury, for preservation. On Monday evening, it was placed in Mr. Shaw's show window for a short time where, as in Wellington, it attracted much attention.

* * * * *

FALL FROM A ROOF

On Thursday evening, a man named Henry Machin, living at 59 New Street, Wellington, was admitted into the Infirmary suffering from a fractured leg, an injury which he received at Wellington the same day by falling from a roof on which he was working.

* * * * *

PRIMITIVE METHODISTS

The Primitive Methodists hereabouts have had quite a high old time of it during the past few days. What with camp meetings, love feasts, processions and other public demonstrations that they have held, the town has been thoroughly lively, and there has been something like a stirring of the dry bones of the denomination in the neighbourhood.

For many years past, Primitive Methodism has held a subordinate position to other denominations in Wellington, but I am certainly of the opinion that the signs of vitality that have been exhibited recently will do something to give it a helpful forward into the more prominent position that it assuredly deserves.

* * * * *

Searching for public houses has long been one of the author's interests. So far, his tally is around the hundred mark. Judging from this report, Dr. Cranage of Old Hall school also had an interest, although he was more concerned with the moral aspect than the historical:

TOO MANY PUBLIC HOUSES?

...The Doctor, it is well known, never goes in for anything by halves. He has calculated the number of public houses in Wellington, and finds they reach the respectable total of sixty, all told.

Thus, it appears, there is one of these 'places of refreshment' to every hundred of the population. Well, I agree with the Doctor that this does appear to be a large number, but I do not think statistics justify us in supposing that if, in a town like Wellington, it were possible to sweep away half of the licensed premises the drink consumed, or the drunkenness propagated, would be less.

In these matters, demand governs the supply, and the same amount of intoxicants would doubtless be consumed whether it came from the taps of one or from those of sixty public houses.

The Doctor said he had been informed by a magistrate, who occupies a seat on the local Bench, that three-fourths of the crime which came before the Tribunal was directly due to drink. I think the magnate in question would have been nearer the mark had he said 'directly due to drunkenness.'

* * * * *

This article reveals how shopkeepers in the town prepared for the seasonal festivities of 1888. Unlike today's Christmas shopping season, which seems to commence at the beginning of September, the first weeks in December marked the start of the 'Christmas rush'. Insofar as food was concerned, the absence of domestic refrigeration and pre-packed ready meals meant that serious shopping didn't really get under way until the week before Christmas Day itself.

CHRISTMAS AT THE SHOPS (1888)

Despite the unseasonable character of the weather, the Christmas Festival at Wellington has been celebrated with quite as much heartiness as in previous years. For days before the event of the Christians' high feast day, the tradesmen of the town exhibited in their establishments evidences of the fact that they were desirous of catering for the wants of any and every customer who desired to celebrate the occasion in an orthodox manner.

Wellington cannot be said to excel in the possession of business premises of striking external pretentiousness, but it may safely lay claim to what is far better, viz., busy and prosperous commercial establishments, and if for fifty and one weeks of the year they devote themselves to the more satisfactory, if less ornamental, form of commerce our tradesmen, when Christmas comes round, are ever ready to show they appreciate the season by those adornments of their premises which take so many and effective shapes, and which have been very conspicuous in the town this season.

A few of the principal shows are all that space will permit me to mention. Let us begin with the butchers, and it may be well to remark that the poultry market on Thursday was one that has rarely ever been equalled, and never excelled, in the town, so far as the quantity and quality of the stock, as well as the number of buyers, were concerned.

The butcher, according to an old-established and, doubtless, a well-warranted custom, appears always to come in for the premier attention at the Christmas market, and there had been a lively competition amongst the local purveyors to excel in the quantity and quality of the stock which they exhibited, as well as in the artistic decorations of their premises. Foremost amongst them were Mr. Beaman of Crown Street and Market Hall, who displayed several prime heifers in a show; Mr. Titley of New Street had some prime Shropshire in his stock, as well as a couple of splendid heifers; Mr. James had a grand show at his establishment in New Street, his exhibition including upwards of a score of grand animals, secured at the leading auctions in the county; The Canterbury Mutton Company made a good display, having no less than 40 sheep in their establishment in New Street; Both Messrs. T.H. and G. Espley made good shows, whilst the shops of Messrs. Juckes, Gallier, Stevens and Dolphin contained ample store of seasonal viands; Mr. A. James, as usual, was to the fore with a prime display of beef and mutton; and Messrs. R. Morgan, Capsey and Webb had each made ample provision to meet the increased demand made upon their resources; Messrs. Bostock and Wyke had also made seasonable provision.

It will be seen from the above that one department of the trading community at any rate recognised the duty they owed to the public at the festive season, and performed it right well. There is small reason to doubt that their efforts were appreciated. But these purveyors were not alone in striving to serve the public wants right royally, for a spirit of generous rivalry appeared to have actuated every tradesman in the town.

The grocers' windows were laden with fruits and spices and all those necessary adjuncts to the Christmas feast which it is their province to supply; the confectioners' stores were simply supplied with many toothsome delicacies which have been in such great demand this week, and which doubtless will continue to be sought after, at this season of the year, so long as Christianity lasts and Christmas is recognised as a time for feasting and merrymaking.

There is another caterer for the public taste which must not be overlooked, viz., the fancy stationer. With these our town is singularly well supplied, but at this particular season of the year they make a brilliant show of Christmas and New Year's cards. These pleasing and inexpensive mementoes of the time appear every year to attain a higher degree of perfection, and many of those displayed this year in the town are of a very high order of artistic merit, and in many cases they display a maximum of elegance and beauty at a minimum of cost.

These are but a few of the principal departments of trade which have, during the past week, helped to make bright and attractive our streets, together with the tasteful adornments which have been executed under the auspices of their proprietors. A few more notable establishments deserve more than a general allusion. Amongst the grocers, those of Messrs. Beaman, G. Lewis (Park Street), J.C. Owen (High Street), J. Hayward (Church Street), Messrs. J.L. and E.T. Morgan (Church Street), Webb Brothers (New Street), the London Tea Co. (New Street), Ison & Co. (New Street), Howes (New Street), J. Birch (King Street) and F. Reece were rendered most conspicuous, both by the nature of the decorations and the quality of stock on hand.

As usual, Messrs. Tudor, Howes and Espley occupied the chief places in the attention of those desiring to purchase confectionery. Mr. J. Bowring had made ample provision to supply all the demands made upon him.

The branch of the Salop Stationery Stores (recently opened at our premises in New Street), as well as the establishments of Mr. Bourne and Mr. Sharman (New Street), Mr. Hobson (Market Square), Mr. Jones (Church Street) and Mr. Swain (New Street) were replete with Christmas and New Year's cards, and presents suitable for the season. Miss Hayward had all the latest music and many fashionable novelties on show at her musical warehouse in Church Street.

Mr. R. Alfred Groom, chairman of the firm at the time this article was written.

The Shropshire Works, Wellington, Salop.—To Railway Waggon Builders, Timber Merchants, Contractors, and Others.—Highly important Sale of exceedingly valuable Freehold PROPERTY, called "The Shropshire Works," comprising Contractors' and Railway Carriage Builders' Premises and Machinery.

MR. WHEATLEY KIRK has the honour to announce that he has been instructed by the assignees of John Dickson and Co. to SELL by AUCTION, at the Bull's Head Inn, Wellington, Salop, on Monday next, the 24th instant, at Four o'clock in the afternoon, in two or such other lot or lots as may be agreed upon, and subject to conditions,

Lot 1. All that Piece or Parcel of Freehold LAND, containing 3a. 1r. 19p., or thereabouts, together with all those very desirable, extensive, and recently erected Premises, called the Shropshire Works, situate at Wellington, Salop, adjoining to the Great Western and London and North-western Railways, to both of which they are connected by permanent rails, comprising all those well-arranged, lofty, and spacious railway carriage building shops, of two storeys high, saw mills, pattern rooms, drying stove, blacksmiths', mechanics', and other workshops, forge, girder making shed, engine shed, and foundry engine, with boiler house, storerooms, and carpenters' shops, well-arranged suites of offices, with convenient fittings and appointments, extensive timber yard, &c.; also the permanent way, or railway, extending throughout the works, and being immediately contiguous and running into the London and North-western and Great Western Railways, and thus communicating with all parts of the United Kingdom. The permanent way comprises 950 yards of malleable iron rails, with points, crossings, and all necessary connections. Also, in this lot, an excellent high-pressure horizontal steam engine, of 22-horse power, capital Cornish boiler, by Galloway, together with all the powerful and exceedingly well fitted shafting, mill gearing steam and water pipes, gas fittings, meters, &c., the whole of which, as having been recently erected, are in the best working condition, and the fires are well adapted for carrying on a large and profitable trade.

2. All that valuable Piece or Parcel of Freehold LAND, adjoining the last lot, as now staked out, formerly known as Lord' Meadow, part of which is now used as a timber and brick yard the remainder an excellent piece of turf, and well adapted for building lots, the whole containing 4a. 0r. 23p. or thereabouts together with a right of road to the same, leading out of the main road from Wellington to or towards Hay Gate, also now or late in the occupation of the said John Dickson and Co.

N.B.—These works are eligibly situated, and adapted for the business for which they are at present arranged, or for any general engineering, foundry, iron, or other works where coal and iron are in request, as both may be obtained in the immediate locality, the works being situated in the centre of the mineral district in Shropshire.

The purchaser of Lot 1 will have the option of taking the whole of the valuable fixed machinery at a valuation, which machinery comprises leviathan stage and travelling crane, brick ovens, Clayton's patent brickmaking machine, completely fitted; Burnetising cylinder and machinery, lathes, punching, shearing, boring, screwing, drilling, planing machines, &c.

Lithographic plans, detailed inventories and particulars, together with any further information, may be had on application to the auctioneer, at his chambers, Cross-street, Manchester; Henry Fisher, Esq., solicitor, Newport, Salop ; R. D. Newill, Esq., solicitor, Wellington, Salop ; and, to view the premises, to Mr. Barber, auctioneer and surveyor, Wellington, Salop.

1856 Sale Notice for The Shropshire Works placed by auctioneers Barbers in The Wellington Journal. *John Dickson & Co. had purchased and built on the site while engaged in the construction of the railway through Wellington together with its subsequent branch lines. Not only was it in an ideal location for developing Groom's timber interests but it also had considerable machinery and, of course, track access to the main railway line which would be of enormous benefit to the firm.*

Chapter 3

R. Groom, Sons & Co. Ltd.

This chapter reproduces an article which appeared in *The Timber Trades Journal* in February 1905 and shows how highly the firm was regarded throughout the country at the peak of its commercial activity.

Representative Home Timber Firms:
R. Groom, Sons & Co., Ltd., Wellington, Salop

There are people, and many of them, even engaged in the timber trade itself, or at least that section of it dealing with imported timber, who look upon the home-grown timber as a very minor, if not almost non-existent, industry scarcely worth a moment's consideration. This erroneous idea probably arises because it is not the rule for huge piles of home grown timber to be in evidence in large depots, such as those met with at our ports in connection with foreign timbers. But the fact that somewhere about £15,000,000 sterling worth of home grown timber comes onto the market annually, and which represents anything from 10 to £15,000,000 sterling after manufacturing and before ultimate consumption, is sufficient to show that it must be handled in large as well as small quantities, and it is our purpose to convey to many of our readers a more accurate idea of the importance and status of the home grown trade, that we are giving illustrated articles of representative home timber firms from time to time.

The well-known firm of R. Groom, Sons & Co. Ltd., of Wellington, Salop, could well lay claim to being representative of practically every section of this diversified business. Without making any invidious comparisons, we might say from our own personal knowledge of most of the principal home timber firms that we are not aware of any other firm in the country so extensively engaged in the conversion and manufacture of every kind of native timber. There is no kind of tree grown but that they can turn to some account, and for which they possess a market. Size is no object to them, for they can handle the largest tree growing in the most awkward position as well as working up to advantage the smallest tree that would in any way come under the usual interpretation of 'timber'. They have often been called in to buy trees which, from their large size and difficulty of position, other merchants have refused to touch, and have not yet been beaten by a job they have undertaken. They have every reason to be proud of a photograph hanging in their offices in Wellington. It represents what was probably the largest oak growing in the country, and which they purchased, and successfully removed and converted. It was felled in Tibberton

Park, almost ten miles from Hereford, in April 1877. The length of the bole, topped at 18 inches diameter, was 88 feet. The whole height of the tree when growing was 130 feet, and the circumference 5 feet from the ground was 22 feet 8 inches, the amount of timber in the tree being 1,200 cubic feet.

The business was founded over 100 years ago by Richard Gregory Groom, grandfather of the present Messrs. Groom, and has thus been in the hands of the same family for three generations, the first proprietor, who commenced the business as a young man, dying in 1865 at the ripe old age of 89.

Among the features connected with the history of the firm, one of much general interest is that they were probably the first users of steam power in the home timber trade in Shropshire, introduced by the late well-known Alderman Richard Groom, of Dothill Park, son of the above R.G. Groom.

This innovation so upset the old man, that he decided to retire from such risky work, leaving his son Richard alone, who then invited his brother Thomas, an engineer in Birmingham, to join, making the firm as known for so many years: R. & T. Groom.

One of the great primary principles recognised in the conduct of this business is efficiency in administration and which, we might explain, by stating that each of the directors is a specialist in his own department; and, as there is no over-lapping, all confusion is avoided, everything being reduced to a perfect system. There are four directors, as under, viz.: Mr. R. Alfred Groom, the chairman, whose portrait we are giving, and who is also the engineer; Mr. Ernest Groom, the finance manager; Mr. W. Edward Groom, outdoor manager, and whose office is 19 Widemarsh Street, Hereford; Mr. Frederick T. Langley, the solicitor, and who is a member of the well-known firm of Fowler, Langley & Wright, solicitors, of Wolverhampton. The site of the present works at Wellington was acquired in 1860.

The business was generally established for the sale of round timber, the converting and manufacturing mills being introduced as a subordinate supplement to this idea to enable the surplus timber left over after the sales of round timber had been effected to be worked up. But this department has grown to such an enormous extent that it now constitutes a huge business in itself.

The premises, though $4^{1/4}$ acres in extent, of which 79,000 square feet represents covered floor space, are well arranged and compact, and are not a whit too large for the business carried on. There are three railway sidings running into the works, two of the late Great Western Railway and one of the London North East Railway, an effective convenience which does away with a vast amount of carrying labour, as trucks can be loaded straight away from the machines themselves without the necessity of long carrying either by crane or hand.

The buildings, which are ranged around the yard, include the offices, the sawing, planing and manufacturing mills; the engine and boiler houses, the drying houses, warehouses and packing rooms.

A huge gantry runs down the middle of the yard, extending 315 feet by 60 feet, and which is served by a large steam over-head travelling crane. The whole available space beneath the crane for the full length of the gantry is occupied with logs, many of them of big dimensions, and include all kinds of timber, from logs of splendid quality oak and ash, to elm and beech and less frequent woods, each particular kind so piled that it can be reached and taken by crane to one of the steam cross-cuts with a minimum loss of time.

To give some idea of the extent of this manifold business, we need only mention that Messrs. Groom can execute orders from heavy dockyard timber down to wooden skewers. For a great number of years they have been large contractors to both the War Office and the Admiralty, as well as to most railway companies in the country. Their huge stock of timber and splendid plant of nearly every description of up-to-date machinery, coupled with their railway siding accommodation on two of the principal railway systems, place them in an unsurpassed position for promptly and efficiently executing the largest orders for home-grown converted timbers of any dimensions.

One secret of the wonderful growth of this business to an unusual, if not unequalled, extent in the English timber trade must be attributed to a sustained determination to master the principles of economical conversion by putting down the very best labour and time-saving appliances, and making use of every possible piece of wood which can be said to possess the slightest commercial value, and it is a system with such obvious results that the slightest doubt cannot exist about the manner in which it has been crowned with the greatest success. And, while we are on this point, we will take a glance at the plan of the premises. It will be seen that the round timber can be brought in by both road and rail - the methods of hauling we are dealing with later - and taken either under the gantry or one of the derricks. When required it is then taken to a power cross-cut (saw) and cut into the required lengths, which are thence taken to a horizontal log band saw, and sawn into flitches or planks that are distributed to all parts of the mill to be further converted and manufactured as may be desired.

The large boiler generating the power for driving the machinery was put down by Galloway & Co., Ltd., of Manchester, and the compound condensing engine was built by Holroyd, Horsfield & Wilson, of Leeds, in 1893, and is of 100 nominal horse power, which means a practical development of 200 horse power when fully at work. All the incomings

Road Locomotive having crane in front and one of the eight-wheel timber carriages. Notice the large gantry and operating cabin above.

and outgoings of this firm are registered to a minute detail, and the water passes through a meter before consumption in the boiler.

The machinery in the mills gives the visitor more of an impression of a big American concern of wood manufacturers than an English timber business. As a rule, a home timber merchant considers himself to be in a fairly good way of business if he has 30 machines running, but Messrs. Groom have as many as 106 machines of all descriptions in continuous work, and this will doubtless point to the advantage of one member of the firm being an engineer. Most of the best British manufacturers of wood-working machinery, and several American makers as well, have supplied their specialities in fitting out this extensive plant and, among them we may mention: Robinson & Son Ltd. of Rochdale; A. Ransome & Co. Ltd. of Newark and London; J. Sagar & Co. Ltd. of Halifax; Cowley & Co. of Bolton; W.A. Fell of Windermere; White & Sons of Paisley; MacDowell & Sons of Glasgow; Baldwin, Tuttill & Co; The Defiance Machine Co.; H.B. Smith & Co, and Greenlees Bros. of America, etc., etc.

It would take up more than the whole of the available space to give details of the different machines supplied by the above firms, and we must content ourselves by just mentioning one or two. One of, if not the most useful machine in the mill, is the large horizontal band saw by A. Ransome & Co. Ltd. It was the second machine of the sort put down by them in this country, and has the distinction of being the first in actual work. As most of our readers are aware, these extremely useful and indispensable machines in such a large mill are capable of an enormous output, and as this one is in constant use every working day from early morning till evening, the amount of work it gets through is really marvellous. Mr. R. Alfred Groom is inventive as well as practical, and as the utmost capacity is demanded from the log band saw, he has improved it by putting in ball bearings, thereby increasing its facility for work in every respect, as we saw while watching it break down some large logs of very tough oak. Amongst the many other machines, some of the most interesting and useful have been invented by Mr. Groom himself. One of these (for turning the legs of washing dollies) struck us as being particularly ingenious, as by a revolving feed about six of these legs are in the machine at a time, and when we mention that

Interior of the Converting Mill showing log band saw.

an average of over 200 dollies are turned out per day, and that each dolly has five legs all turned by this machine, it will be easily imagined what a useful and expeditious appliance this is. Another machine (also invented by Mr. Groom) used for cutting up firewood is so constructed that it makes six cuts in one operation by means of an arrangement of circular saws, and quickly reduces a large heap of rough slabs to short lengths, which at this time of the year are loaded straight into trucks and sent away by rail every day, thus avoiding an accumulation that would quickly reach alarming proportions in a business where such immense quantities of timber are dealt with daily.

One of the main features upon which the success of this firm has been built up and is maintained is the implicit confidence that their customers possess in knowing that they can absolutely depend upon the fact that any manufactured goods they buy are perfectly seasoned. No expense has been spared in the construction of several large drying sheds upon the best and most efficient principles, and the wood, after being cut to proper sizes, with, of course, the necessary allowances for shrinkage, is stacked for twelve, eighteen or twenty-four months, or longer if required, until every vestige of moisture has disappeared; and, by the way, in one large shed alone we were shown over 600,000 pieces of timber thus stacked to season.

Natural drying is chiefly adhered to, although for urgent orders for seasoned material three large drying kilns have been built for finishing the process, these being heated with live steam from the boiler.

As with the machinery, so with the hundreds of specialities supplied by Messrs. Groom, they would take up the whole of the space at our command to enumerate. They have laid themselves out to supply in any quantities every description of heavy converted timbers,

Interior of the Manufacturing Mill showing a few of the machines in operation.

such as dockyard timbers and timbers used in large constructive works; wagon scantlings; all kinds of planks and scantlings; fencing materials, gates and gate-posts; wheelwrights' materials, such as naves, shafts, felloes, and spokes, quartered and bastard oak, and elm, coffin boards, barrow materials, and ladder rounds, &c., &c.

In their lighter, and what could have been more specifically described as their manufactured specialities, we may briefly mention a few as under, viz.: Compressed oak railway keys, D eye and crutch, straight and bent, shovel and spade handles (in parenthesis we might mention that they supply the War Office with large quantities of bent trees, which must on no account be fractured in the bending), peggy and chump washing dollies (these are being manufactured at the rate of eight to ten gross per week), wood measures readily ironed and Government stamped in all sizes ranging from a bushel to a half-pint, wood seed hoppers, hair sieves in all sizes, riddle and sieve rims, turned sycamore or willow bowls, every imaginable kind of dairy and domestic wood utensils, from a milking stool skimming dish, or step ladder to a mouse trap, potato and malt shovels, wood taps, mole traps, hay rakes, hay fork and scythe handles, pick shafts, axe and hammer handles, sack trucks, peels, wagon and cart bows, and tub and bucket hoops, brushmakers' woodware, &c., &c.

The timber for keeping this business supplied with its raw material must obviously be procured over a very wide area, and it is needless to remark that the quantity is both varied and immense. A radius of at least 100 miles in all directions from Wellington is laid under contribution, and large consignments are also imported from Ireland and abroad. It is necessary in localities at long distance from Wellington for the timber to be hauled to the nearest station by local hauliers, but at the same time Messrs. Groom are well provided for hauling in by road over considerable distances. In this, as in other respects, they are well up to date, and even in some ways may be said to be pioneers in the home timber trade. For the work they do themselves they have a road locomotive (specially built for their requirements by the well-known makers of road locomotives, Fowler & Co. Ltd., Leeds) capable of doing the work of thirty horses. It is fitted in front with a crane that will lift five tons.

Equipped with this crane and a long wire cable, it can drag the timber through a wood, and from sites unapproachable by horses can load its own trucks, haul them home, and unload if necessary, thus dispensing entirely with horses, although a considerable number of these useful animals are kept for the lighter journeys and other work. The broad wheeled carriages used in connection with the locomotive are probably of a unique design, as instead of the usual four they have eight wheels. This additional number of wheels spare the roads and prevent any serious friction with the local authorities, the amount of weight allowed under the Act controlling the use of road locomotives being a maximum of 4 tons 13 cwts, to a pair of wheels, thus, by a proper distribution of weight, permitting a comparatively heavy load without infringement. As four trucks are in use no delay occurs in unloading, as two trucks only are hauled by the locomotive at a time.

As we have intimated before, the business in round timber is also very extensive, considerable quantities being sold direct, either from growing site, or hauled to station, to buyers in the round. The photograph we are giving of a large brown oak tree will serve to show what the firm is capable of doing in the way of hauling. It lay in a very awkward position, but was dragged by the engine cable across a ploughed field, was loaded, hauled, and unloaded at the entrance to the yard at Wellington, where it was photographed. We might mention that it measured 12 feet in diameter at the butt end.

The distribution of the converted timbers and manufactured goods is necessarily of the highest importance. Many of the latter are exported direct to the Colonies and foreign countries, while travellers cover the whole of the ground from Glasgow to the South Coast, and also Ireland from Dublin to Belfast.

In addition to the home-grown timber business, Messrs. Groom carry on a considerable local trade in foreign timber, principally builders' goods.

In conclusion, we must express our regret that the limited space at our command only allows us to do merely superficial justice to the great industry represented by the name of R. Groom, Sons, & Co., Ltd., but we are confident that our readers who are interested in the home timber trade will agree with us in renewing their hope for the future of home timber when they realise what even now can be done by a strict observance of those business principles and systems to which Messrs. Groom have so closely adhered during their long and successful career.

Large brown oak hauled to and laid down outside the yard at Wellington.

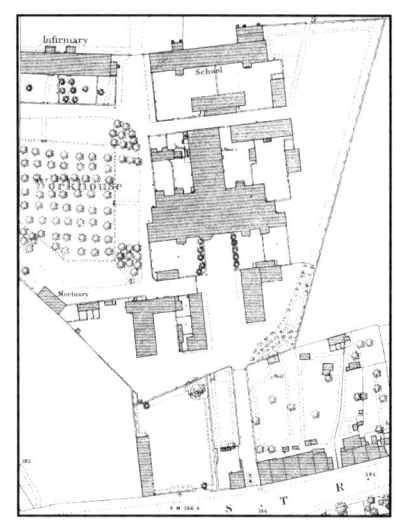

Plan of Wellington Workhouse grounds, 1882. It had its own mortuary, infirmary and school for pauper children. Separate accommodation for men and women inevitably led to families being split up.

Below: Sketch of Apley Castle as printed in The Wellington Standard, 1889. The description given was: 'The handsome mansion is built of brick with stone facings in the Italian style; the principal entrance is through a massive Roman portico supported by eight columns. The approach from the main road is by a stone lodge; the drive extends a mile through a well wooded park. On the right is a piece of ornamental water, almost hidden by the thick foliage; elms and chestnuts thrive in abundance, and in the park are to be seen some of the finest cattle in Shropshire. A neatly kept drive, hedged with yew and bordered with beautiful pines and sycamore trees leads to the stables... the effect is very striking.' Apley Castle was home to Thomas Meyrick, a leading figure in town affairs and well aware of his position in society but who was not universally popular among townsfolk.

Chapter 4

Officialdom in 1889

Those people who put themselves forward for public office often seem full of their own self-importance and have a strong conviction that their opinions are always right. Unfortunately, the truth is seldom so clear-cut. Public officialdom is not always in tune with public opinion, especially where the law governing their actions is concerned. A few articles, again taken from *The Wellington Standard*, show just how much resentment can be generated when those sitting on public bodies lose touch with common sense or seek to excuse their actions by hiding behind laws which are unfair, out-dated or too restrictive.

It's surprising how such views still hold true. Modern councils and the attitudes of their employees don't seem to have improved overmuch in more than a century.

NEW STREET PAVEMENTS
If you have passed up the thoroughfare of New Street this week you will have noticed that the repavement of the footpaths has begun. I am delighted to have noticed this outburst of parochial energy and, with a hundred more who beheld it on Wednesday last, I fairly chortled in my joy. I cannot hold my peace, I must give vent to my feelings, for if I did not the stones themselves would cry out: 'Hurrah! Hurrah!'

* * * * *

BURIAL SCANDALS
EDITORIAL
That was a wonderfully pathetic story told by the Rev. J. Judson at the Board of Guardians meeting on Thursday last of a father taking his child to the grave in a wheelbarrow, owing to the fact that he was unable to obtain suitable appliances for the interment to be made in a decent and orderly manner. But the story appeals not alone to the pathetic, for it appears to me to demonstrate the fact, and to demonstrate it very forcibly, too, that there is not plenty of provision made in the town for giving the poorer classes those privileges which they have a right, as ratepayers, to demand of those who hold the strings of the public purse.

Far be it from my desire, in a question of this kind, to endeavour to create ill-feeling between the poor and our more fortunate fellow townsmen; but who, possessing those feelings of common humanity, can contemplate to witness such a spectacle as the one that Mr. Judson was subjected to?

Such strong feelings of revulsion resulted in further discussions. Differing views showed how some members of the Board of Guardians (Edward Lawrence in particular: he later served as Master of the Workhouse for a short while until ejected from the position for showing humanitarian tendencies) were more in touch with public opinion than others (like Richard Groom who, being perhaps the most influential businessmen in the town at that time, disliked the prospect of losing face and certainly didn't relish the thought of his decisions coming under public scrutiny).

The Board of Guardians took their duties seriously, too seriously on occasion, especially when endeavouring not to spend ratepayers' money unnecessarily (in their eyes). Upon reading the reports, the word 'jobsworth' springs to mind, as do modern bureaucratic techniques of absolving guilty parties of blame. Another point worth mentioning is that the 'parish hearse' referred to was certainly not a glass-sided carriage complete with black horses wearing black ostrich plumes so favoured by the middle classes; it was, in fact, little more than a long trolley or cart with handles. Furthermore, Mr. Groom's opposition to providing the town with a mortuary in addition to the one at the Workhouse was probably influenced more by a desire not to spend money unnecessarily than a fear of spreading disease. Obviously, good citizens would rather die than have their corpse moved into the mortuary at the Workhouse where it could find itself lying next to a lowly pauper!

When the Board of Guardians (comprising Mr. R. Groom (in the chair), Messrs. Lawrence and Instone (vice-chairmen), Mr. France-Hayhurst (ex-officio), the Rev. T. Owen, J. Judson, William Sabben, and a Mr. A. P. Salusbury, and Messrs. Taylor, Hopley, Williams, Shakeshaft, and Leighton) met, they discussed three cases where the authorities had let bereaved families down terribly. Some, like Richard Groom, dug their heels in, regarding the current laws as rigid and to be adhered to at all costs. Edward Lawrence took a more humane view and criticised the officers of the Board whose inefficiency and obstructiveness had caused so much grief. He raised the valid point that, just because someone cannot afford to pay for medicines prescribed by the Board's medical officer, it did not make him a pauper, and pointed out that the rules specifically said so.

Other Board members were equally rattled by the upsurge of public opinion against actions carried out on the Board's behalf. They agreed with Mr. Lawrence in that it 'was a monstrous thing that in a town like Wellington two dead bodies should have been kept in houses where they should certainly not have been permitted to remain longer than was absolutely unavoidable. Why did they not have a mortuary?' Mr. Groom objected to a mortuary being erected near the centre of the Wellington as it might bring all sorts of disease into the town. He went on to say that, although the Board must accept responsibility for its recent shortcomings, no blame should be attached to Mr. Thomas, the Master of the Workhouse.

The sorry tale didn't end there. Wellington's residents were incensed to discover what had happened, not just once but on several occasions in recent weeks. It became the talk of the town, so much so that the subject was discussed at one of Wellington's foremost debating societies of the period:

THE CROWN DEBATING SOCIETY DISCUSS THE SUBJECT
At the weekly meeting of the Crown Debating Society held in the Club Room at the Crown Inn (in Crown Street), Wellington last night, the subject selected for discussion was 'The Recent

Burial Disgrace'. Mr. Molyneux occupied the chair, and there was a fair attendance of members present.

Mr. Williams, of The Stores, opened the debate. He said the child, he believed, was taken bad on Saturday, and they went to the relieving officer to get an order for the doctors, but when the order was obtained a delay occurred. The doctor ordered treatment, but the people had no money to purchase the articles required. They asked for relief to purchase them and it was refused, but the owner of the lodging-house eventually advanced 6d, which was spent on poultices and other remedies ordered. After the death of the child, Mr. Taylor, the Nuisance Inspector, came to the place and wanted the father to pay some men to take the child to the cemetery. The woman asked Mr. Taylor to pay the men, but he refused to do so, and afterwards came up and brought two drunks and women with him, and said she must pay them for taking the child to the grave. Mrs. Moore said that she would not pay them as she had done all she could for the family by relieving them. Mr. Taylor then said, 'If you do not send the child out of your house by the time appointed, I will stick a paper in your window and charge you a shilling for every half hour you detain the corpse on the premises.'

Then the father said if he could have a decent wheelbarrow he would bury it himself. Mrs. Moore then came to him (the speaker) and asked if he would please to lend a wheelbarrow, and he said decidedly he would, and asked to see the father whom he recognised as a decent and respectable man, and he and Mr. Collins gave him some refreshment before he went to wheel the child. Mr. Collins said the father then put a cloth under and over the coffin, and tied it so that it would not shift about, and the father bowled his own child to the cemetery, and then returned the wheelbarrow to him.

He (the speaker) had been to the United States of America for six years, he had been in New York, Texas, Kansas, Nebraska, Ohio, &c., but he had never witnessed such a thing in all the days of his life. Where there was hardly anybody about he had known when a death had taken place that the residents had flocked to the place and taken the corpse to the grave on wagons where a hearse could not be obtained. From what he had recently witnessed he should say that even in those wilds the people were more cultivated than in England.

Mr. Growcott, who followed, pointed out that there was a contradiction between the statement made by Mr. Taylor and the one published in the Wellington Journal, in which paper it was stated that Mr. Taylor had offered to pay men to carry the coffin; it now appeared he had not done so, but had desired Mrs. Moore to do so. He would like the position of the sanitary officer to be distinctly laid down. The event must give rise in the breast of any man with an atom of humanity to the utmost indignation. The guardians evidently did not know that they were responsible and that society had, therefore, a right to make enquiries and endeavour to elucidate the subject.

Mr. Casewell said it appeared from what they had heard that the public officials were not the only uncharitable persons in the town. A member then pointed out that at the time of this occurrence there was a difference of opinion as to which authority was responsible but this had since been cleared up. The Guardians recognised that they were responsible if a man was in receipt of medical attendance to put the body in a coffin, but it was a moot point if they were also responsible for for its being carried to the grave.

Mr. T Steventon said it appeared to them that a man was a pauper if he was receiving out-relief in money or in kind, but if a man had any medicine, attendance, or other necessaries recommended by the parish doctors, these things did not debar him voting, and if they did not affect his right as a voter why should they pauperise him? Mr. Growcott said he was pleased to hear that the matter was getting cleared up, and it was very necessary that every public officer should understand his responsibility. Of course, if a corpse was left in a house long enough, the householder became responsible, as it became a nuisance, but if the officers of the Board had understood their duties this would probably never have occurred. It was now distinctly understood that the poor law officers were in such cases responsible for putting the body in a coffin if not for carrying it to the grave.

Mr. Casewell failed to see that according to the law that parish medical aid made a man a pauper. He thought that in a town in a great nation like ours, if there were not two men to be found to carry a corpse to the grave without the sanitary officers having to canvass the town from end to end, it was a scandal. A member said he had been told that there were women in the town who were ready to volunteer to carry the corpse to the grave.

Mr. Jenkinson said the question that had to be decided was, who was to deal with the evil in the event of it occurring again? They had had scandals in regard to burials in Wellington before, and it was not so long since that a coffin was buried empty, and the corpse left in the mortuary. It was shame that there were four bodies in the town with power to levy rates, and that there was no one to see that the work was done properly.

Mr. Growcott said that there appeared to be no doubt that Mr. Newman would, in the future, have to superintend the business in cases where parish relief was given, but if a death took place in the town where parish relief had not been given, it fell upon the Board of Commissioners to bury the body, and it could only be moved by requisitioning the parish hearse, and the authorities would only lend the hearse in the event of the Commissioners' officer superintending the arrangements. This he refused to do, and so they were faced with a further difficulty. A member: then the responsibility falls upon the person who owns the house in which a party dies.

Mr. Jackson then proposed the following resolution, which was seconded by Mr. Steventon, and carried nem. con.: 'That in the opinion of this society the Commissioners should instruct their inspector in all cases of deaths other than paupers in destitute circumstances, that he apply for the use of the parish hearse, and to see it safely returned.'

It was also suggested that a public meeting be called to draw the attention of the ratepayers to the facts of the case, one of the members remarking that the case was being widely commented upon outside the limits of the county, and in Shrewsbury it was common talk.

A further vote was passed by the society expressing the deep regret of members at the circumstances attending the death and burial of the child, and the hope that such an event would never take place in the town again. Mr. Shaw, in seconding the motion, stated that he was pleased to have the opportunity of saying that there were those in the town who had some sympathy with the poor in their distress. Mr. Hobson (the chairman of the Board of Commissioners) sent, per Mr. Edwardes, to the society to say that the Board accepted the responsibility with respect to persons dying who were not paupers to bury them and to pay the burial fees.

The *Wellington Standard*, as if to emphasise the bias given in reports by the *Wellington Journal*, included this in its Editorial a week later:

...Looking back at the events of last week, one finds much to reflect upon. Foremost amongst them, of course, was the burial scandal at Wellington. I really had so much to say in regard to the extraordinary proceedings that took place in the town a fortnight ago that I am almost afraid of wearying my readers by again referring to the subject. In some quarters, however, I am told I am guilty of pandering to the sentimental and playing to the gallery, oblivious of the fact that 'law is law' and that the officers of the various authorities in the town have to carry out the law, and not to be influenced by feelings of compassion in particular cases.

I must protest against these attempts to close discussion on the subject. It has been proved that the public of the town, or that portion of the public least able to protect itself, has a palpable and a crying grievance. This must be remedied! It is no use saying there are insurmountable obstacles in the way, they must be removed. What occurred a fortnight ago may otherwise occur again.

We have heard an outcry, and one not made altogether without reason, against those who placed obstacles in the way of the burial of a poor child in Ireland, but if such scenes as have been lately witnessed in Wellington are to be repeated, if aid is refused here to the sorrowing parents to bury their dead, we shall soon have little reason to upbraid our Irish cousins.

* * * * *

Not all *Standard* reports were quite so damning or so highly critical of local government and, where possible, the editor tried to find an element of humour when publishing his observations.

CANNON DEFENCE GETS SHOT DOWN

I went to the Wellington Police Court on Monday, not for amusement but to see even-handed justice meeted out to all and sundry who had been unlucky enough to come under the eagle eye of the law. I say I did not go to be amused and yet, when John Cannon stepped into the dock he conveyed a ray of humour. John was charged with stealing six cauliflowers from the garden of Mr. Newill who, by the way, is clerk to the Bench. A police man found the cauliflowers at his house, when the defendant admitted to him that he had purloined the vegetables. He, however, withdrew this statement, and defied the 'noblemen of the Bench to convict him.' Then he proceeded to make as much noise as half-a-dozen well regulated cannons, and told 'their noble lordships' a pretty tale about the cauliflowers being thrown over his garden wall. He always concluded his argument in the same strain, thusly, 'Noblemen, you cannot convict me, because nobody saw me take them.'

The Bench, nevertheless, refused to recognise their incapacity, and they did convict Mr. Cannon, who will, doubtless, take a broader view of the law, and the powers thereof, in the future.

* * * * *

Boxing Day always presented a dilemma to tradesmen in late Victorian times, especially since it was not a traditional public holiday. Should they do the decent thing and let employees have the day off (unpaid) to spend with their families, or insist on them turning up for work as usual, in order that sales could continue unhindered?

BOXING DAY CLOSING

There appears to be considerable confusion existing in the minds of tradesmen of the town as to what course they will pursue in regard to closing their respective business establishments on Boxing Day.

This, I think, is partly due to the fact that there has been no concerted action amongst the shopkeepers as a whole, and consequently I expect to see a portion of the shops opened, whilst the remainder are closed.

This uncertainty might have easily been obviated had some authoritative request been addressed to the whole of the tradesmen, say from the chairman of the Improvement Commissioners on behalf of that body, and I think to have sent such a request would have been a very wise course of action to have pursued in the circumstances. Of course, it is too late now to do anything in the matter, but the suggestion is worth entertaining for application in years to come.

* * * * *

LOCAL GOVERNMENT SECRECY

I have not been able to ascertain yet what the Wellington Improvement Commissioners have decided to do in regard to the re-arrangement of the duties of the inspector of nuisances and the surveyor. They met to consider the subject in camera on Wednesday week, and there have been several rumours current as to the result of their deliberations, the one that is most generally accepted being that Mr. Taylor, the nuisance inspector, will in future be expected to act under the supervision of Mr. Reid, the surveyor. I only give this rumour, however, for what it is worth.

Another matter discussed by the same meeting with closed doors, I am creditably informed, was the financial condition of the Board. Now I do not wish, for a moment, to cast any aspersion upon the wisdom of the gentlemen who control the public affairs of this town, and hold the purse strings of the ratepayers, but I do think it is only right that those who pay the piper should know what is being done with their money; and no public body, however immaculate, has a right to prevent their masters (for the ratepayers are their masters) from being fully acquainted with the truth, and the whole truth, as to their financial position.

* * * * *

Without having a proper hospital or mortuary in the town, post mortem examinations usually took place in the deceased's home, where the body would be laid out for visitors to pay their last respects before the funeral. Inquests were held at a nearby public house.

SHOCKING SUICIDE AT WELLINGTON

An inquest was held at the Buck's Head Inn, Watling Street, Wellington, by Mr. J.V.T. Lander and a jury of which Mr. Wollenstein was the foreman, touching the death of Eliza Corbett, aged

32, late of Arleston.

Enoch Corbett (father of the deceased) identified the body as that of his daughter. She had left home at nine on Saturday morning in the company of two little girls. From what he afterwards learned, she left the two children at the bottom of the lane near the Buck's Head, having kissed them goodbye. He never saw her alive afterwards. She was always complaining that she had 'back-slidden' and could get no peace, but otherwise she was in good health, although she had been attended by Dr. Calwell. He went with a man in search of his daughter and eventually he found her in the Warehouse Pool at Ketley.

James Briscoe, engine driver, Arlestone, corroborated. He said that he had had frequent conversations with the deceased, who stated that she had sinned, and there was no forgiveness for her. He found the body in the pool, in about 18 inches of water.

Mrs. Emily Owen, who wore the uniform of the Salvation Army, said that she knew the deceased very well, and that she was at her house the whole of Friday afternoon, and appeared to be particularly distressed about her soul being lost. Deceased said she had fallen into sin and could not find pardon, and witness told her she must not give way to the suggestions of the Evil One, in reply to which the deceased said she could not trust God because she had spurned his mercy. Deceased afterwards told her that she could get no sleep at night, and had troubled dreams.

PC Woosnam gave evidence as to the finding of the body, and the jury returned a verdict of 'Suicide whilst temporarily insane'.

* * * * *

While on the subject of insanity (always a good fall-back diagnosis when actions have no sensible explanation), the Board of Guardians found it difficult to get help when lunatic paupers (they were always paupers) had to be transported to the Asylum at Shrewsbury. The author's great grandfather John Jones was Clerk to the Board and placed this advertisement in the *Wellington Standard*. Incidentally, Mr. Jones was also responsible for handing 'outdoor relief' dole payments to folk who weren't so poor as to necessitate incarceration in the Workhouse. He did this through a window to the right of the door to Gwynne's solicitors in Walker Street, where the Board's office was then situated.

WELLINGTON (SALOP) UNION

TO POSTMASTERS, INNKEEPERS, AND OTHERS: *Persons desirous of CONTRACTING for the CONVEYANCE of PAUPER LUNATICS from this Union to Bicton Asylum for Twelve Months, are requested to send in TENDERS for the same to my office not later than Five o'clock on WEDNESDAY, the 14th day of August instant. The Contractor will be required to provide a Close Carriage, Pair of Horses or Single (at his option), and Driver; the sum named to include all expenses connected therewith, and must Convey the Patient and necessary Attendants to the Asylum from any part of Wellington Relief District and the Attendants back again. The whole arrangements to be under the direction of the Relieving Officer.*

* * * * *

Members of official public bodies did, despite some failings, have Wellington's interests at heart. As well as improving basic amenities, such as maintaining pavements and ensuring regular supplies of clean water piped from the reservoirs at the foot of The Wrekin Hill to standpipes dotted around at various locations, it also sought to improve the town's reputation. It was something of a feather in the cap to be chosen to host the Shropshire and West Midlands Agricultural Show, which took place on land (now occupied by Wrekin College at the top of Constitution Hill) which was then owned by Thomas Meyrick of Apley Castle. The whole town got caught up in the excitement of the event, as this *Wellington Standard* report of 1889 clearly shows:

SHROPSHIRE & WEST MIDLAND AGRICULTURAL SHOW

The first exhibition that has been held under the joint auspices of various societies comprising the Shropshire & West Midlands Agricultural Show was opened at Wellington yesterday. The approaches to the ground on Constitution Hill were gaily decorated with flags and bunting, and the town generally had put on quite a brilliant appearance to welcome the advent of the society to the town. In New Street, most of the places of business bore appropriate flags and devices on their facades, converting the thoroughfare into an avenue of fluttering bunting. All of the tradesmen exhibited, in some form or other, their welcome to the exhibition, and the Square, Church Street, Station Road and other parts of the town were specially conspicuous in this respect.

On Tuesday night, a considerable number of visitors came to the town and the streets were quite lively with those desiring to view the decorations. At the Charlton Arms, considerable attention was attracted by the illumination of the front of the building with the electric light. The Wrekin Hotel, Station Hotel and, in fact, all the public houses in the town exhibited flags or banners.

Bayley's College on Constitution Hill, near to the show ground, had strings of banners across the roof. The entrance to the show yard is most conveniently situated, and every possible arrangement has been made in order to facilitate the exit and entry of visitors. Rapid progress has been made in the inclosure during the last few days, and when the gates were thrown open to the public at 9 o'clock yesterday morning, everything on the ground was in excellent order, and if, here and there, there were additions or completions to be made, an hour or two's work set all this right.

The recent dry weather has served to make the surface of the enclosure in a condition to render locomotion not only easy but enjoyable. The morning opened cloudy but fine, with a cool breeze blowing over the show yard, the general appearance of the morning giving every promise that, so far as atmospheric surroundings are concerned, the show of 1889 will be no wise inferior to any of the previous Shropshire exhibitions.

Nothing could possibly be more satisfying to the well-wishers of the show than the number of entries, which are as follows: Horses, 231; Cattle, 212; Sheep, 178; Pigs, 37; Butter, cheese and wool, 76. Compared with last year, these numbers show a decided increase, the total number of entries in 1888 being 695. It is a remarkable fact that last year the numbers of sheep were in excess of those on show this year, the number shown in 1888 being 227.

* * * * *

Chapter 5

Pictures from the Past

The author never ceases to be amazed at the amount of information hidden away in boxes and battered old suitcases in lofts, attics, beneath beds and inside wardrobes. Many people don't even realise what treasures they have tucked away, neglected and forgotten.

It is a shame that very few folk bother to answer appeals for information; without help from the general public, a considerable amount of information is cast away without a second thought. Much of it cannot be replaced. A single photograph or other document may not have monetary value but it could well add knowledge to our understanding of Wellington's history.

These hidden treasures are of extreme importance to the author, who encourages everyone to help by letting him borrow them for a short while; it is very difficult to write history books without them. Please venture into the deepest recesses of your home to fish out anything, however insignificant it may seem, to help him continue his work.

The Lodge to Apley Castle, seen here in the early 1960s. The castle was sold in the early 1950s and later demolished. The Princess Royal Hospital, several factories and housing estates now occupy the grounds.

The Cock Hotel crossroads, seen here without traffic lights, 1960s, with the Swan Hotel (built in 1960) on the left. The vertical 'Raleigh' sign on the wall to the right marks Harry Sutch's bike shop.

Crossroads at the Buck's Head, early 1950s, with a British Railways delivery lorry emerging from Haybridge Road (left) and a Corona pop wagon turning into Arleston Lane to make home deliveries.

The former Clifton Cinema and Saverite supermarket, mid-1960s. Both now comprise Dunelm soft furnishing store. The Ercall Works warehouse on the left had previously been G.E. Turner's gunsmiths, seed, fertiliser and feedstuff merchants, an indication that he served the needs of the farming community.

Crown Street, mid-1960s, showing The Fox and Hounds public house on the right.

The Priory, former Georgian vicarage to All Saints parish church, falls victim to new housing, late 1960s. The name of the building is preserved in Priory Close, one of the streets created on the site.

Houses in Foundry Road were demolished in the early 1980s...

... as was Bernie Pugh's s Antiques shop. It had formerly been a general stores run by Beatrice Mansell.

With Foundry Road no more than a mere memory, work begins on creating a public car park on the site.

Frost's Bakery (chimney, right) at the top of New Street about to be demolished, early 1970s. To the left is Ward's newsagents and Tim Briscoe's butchers shop; the latter had previously been run by Jack Nicholls.

Towards the top of New Street, 1960s, with the Council car park on the left and Frank Sansom's former furniture shop on the right hand corner. Victoria Road now cuts through this section.

Above: O. D. Murphy's Wrekin Mineral Waters ('Pop') Works (originally the Shropshire Brewery), mid-1970s, demolished by the Telford Development Corporation in order to build houses on this historic site. Below: The Gas Works in the mid-1960s, when it processed coal to produce coke and town gas. Visitor tours were often held here to enlighten the general public and reveal how by-products were used to make a variety of useful items, such as aspirins and ladies stockings (tights were just coming into fashion at that time). Coke was sold to local coal merchants as many households preferred to burn fuel which emitted less smoke than coal itself and, it was argued, was capable of reaching higher temperatures.

Demolition work gets under way of sidings at the Wellington Town Goods Depot railway warehouse on the southern side of the track, mid-1960s. Note the gas holder full of town gas before natural gas from the North Sea replaced it; the holder was manufactured and erected by C. & W. Walker of the Midland Iron Works, Donnington, a firm which specialised in building such structures throughout the world.

Part of Glebe Street was flattened to enable the erection of Government Buildings, a new Department of Health & Social Security office, mid-1960s. The Chad Valley Wrekin Toy Works dominates the centre of the photograph.

View from Constitution Hill looking towards the Ercall and Wrekin hills, 1960s. New Street Methodist Church (centre left), which dominated this part of the town when built in 1882, was demolished in November 2003 to make way for a modern church building. Wright's grocery shop (bottom centre) on the corner of King Street and Victoria Street was a popular port of call for sweet-seeking children attending Constitution Hill school.

Rear view of The Villa in Church Street, 1952. Built as a desirable Victorian town house with an extensive garden, the grounds have since been replaced by buildings and a car park. The house is now used as an office by Lanyons solicitors. It had formerly been the surgery for Drs. Thompson and Hewatt-Jaboor.

Foundations are prepared for new swimming baths, early 1980s, while Wellington's original public baths (left, built in 1910), counts the days before demolition.

District of The Wrekin planners outraged local residents, not just of Wellington but every township comprising the Telford conurbation, when they erected town signs incorporating an icon of the Iron Bridge, thus confirming their ignorance of the district's history and arrogance towards the sensitivities of ratepayers. Such signs became targets of justified 'vandalism' by incensed locals until the icon was officially removed.